My
MENTOR
My
HEALER

MARTHA FRANKSON

WestBow Press books may be ordered through booksellers or by contacting:

WestBow Press
A Division of Thomas Nelson & Zondervan
1663 Liberty Drive
Bloomington, IN 47403
www.westbowpress.com
844-714-3454

Because of the dynamic nature of the Internet, any web addresses or links contained in this book may have changed since publication and may no longer be valid. The views expressed in this work are solely those of the author and do not necessarily reflect the views of the publisher, and the publisher hereby disclaims any responsibility for them.

Any people depicted in stock imagery provided by Getty Images are models, and such images are being used for illustrative purposes only.
Certain stock imagery © Getty Images.

Scripture taken from the King James Version of the Bible.

ISBN: 979-8-3850-3628-8 (sc)
ISBN: 979-8-3850-3631-8 (hc)
ISBN: 979-8-3850-3632-5 (e)

Library of Congress Control Number: 2024921756

Print information available on the last page.

WestBow Press rev. date: 3/11/2025

WESTBOW
PRESS®
A DIVISION OF THOMAS NELSON
& ZONDERVAN

To my husband, Ira Frankson Sr.

And our beautiful family
Helen, Crystal, Ira jr, Claudia,
Annette, Maxine, Emma

Ebrulik, Angelica, Trona, Kendra, Abraham, Leo
Kobe, Jaden, Brayden, Franklin,
Aaliyah, Andrew, Ira the 3rd, Seymour, Lucy
Rebecca, Ben Jr., Jacob, Joanna, Matthew, Gloria, Ariella, Josiah
Milton Jr
Charla, Anna, Akivgaluk, Qalayuaq, Martha

Zoey, Renezmae, Lucas

Ray, Ben Sr. and Leon

Psalms 147:3 He healeth the broken in heart, and bindeth up their wounds.

I was sitting here at the Kotzebue airport waiting to board a plane when I got a call from one of the ladies working in Manilaq. "Martha, they want you to stay here your son been hit with a car. A broken leg they are bringing him here". My heart sank my baby, my son my 4-year-old. I escorted a baby this morning to Kotzebue from my hometown Point Hope. The next call came a few minutes later something about they want you to go home. My question did he not make it?

I was born on a cold winter night might have been in the early AM, when everyone was asleep. My mom went into labor and my dad had to get a midwife the well known one of Point Hope. He walked to their home and knocked on the door for awhile no one answered the door. So he finally called her name then said in Inupiaq my wife is in labor. She got up as fast as she can and said we didn't answer the door because there was a drunk lady bothering us all night and we thought it was her knocking again. They went to our house and I was born already. My grandma Lily delivered me and my sister Grace assisted by looking for the scissors and handing it to my grandma. So this story of my being born was told over and over to me and we always end up laughing because of the drunk lady. My life growing up in Point Hope was a good life. At least I thought it was good. I come from a family of nine kids and 2 adopted. I was the fifth child, four older than me and six younger than me.

Our dad was a good provider, always hunting in Point Hope or working in Kotzebue as a maintenance he also was in the National Guard and in the Alaska

Territorial Guard. My mom worked in Kotzebue at Hanson and Rotman's also babysat for Margie at Kotzebue.

When living in Point Hope my dad always made sure we ate a good meal. My mom and dad hunted year around and gathered food too. My dad would always get up early in the morning, always had to be early. Like in early bird catches the worm. In the winter he would go hunt seals on the ice, go hunt caribou on land towards the mountains or to go hunt wolves, foxes or wolverine. While we are still sleeping, I can hear dad getting ready must be like 6am or earlier maybe later. We would be sleeping on the floor in sleeping bags early on we had beds before the house burned. Then later when we moved to the other house for a while we slept on the floor until my parents bought a bed. I can hear the dogs barking as my dad harnesses the dogs to go hunting. In the wintertime when he would go hunting and it would still be dark outside, so I really didn't know what time he got up.

One time he came home with a wolf my first time to ever see one it was so big I asked: "Is that a horse?" My parents laughed at what I said. Those days we would all be so happy, always together. He would come home late sometimes and many times when he came home, I remember him sitting by the table eating after a long day hunting my sister Helen would grab dad's hand and use his hand as a doll and pretend to be packing his hand as packing a baby. I remember doing that to dad once and as tired as he is he never complained, my dad was so patient. We did this while he's sitting by the

table talking to mom about his day after a good meal. He'd leave early in the morning and come home late at night, sometimes he'd come home early. When he came home from hunting, he'd always have to tie the dogs up and put whatever he catches in the house. If he caught a seal, I remember we'd have to give the seal water or sometimes I'd see a small piece of saltine cracker in the opening of the dead seal's mouth. Something about feeding the spirit and the seal or animal would come back, because the family treated them good. If my dad and mom had enough seals to last, they always shared it with family and friends who needed some food or seal blubber for heat in the stove. Point Hope people made stoves out of 55-barrel drums before the store-bought cooking stove. My mom and dad had a cook stove the kind you use stove oil.

My dad and mom gathered food too, berries in August, blueberries and salmon berries. They sometimes gathered shrimp and worms from the beach, after a storm they'd go to the beach and look for them. I remember many times they would come home with worms from the beach, shrimp and what not. I never really tried any of it. Mom would ask me if I wanted to try some, and I didn't really want to try any of it.

Life for them was always on the go, my mom would sew parkas for my dad, us kids and for herself. She would sew maklaks (Inupiaq boots) for the family. Dad would have a warm parka for hunting. Usually, the white cloth covered the warm mouton skin and that's used for hunting, working outside in the winter or spring dad would have a mouton parka covered with a dark cloth like blue or black. When my mom sewed for us, it would be for whaling feast or Christmas. She'd make parkas and maklaks.

She'd have a warm parka for herself to carry baby on the back or for visiting her lady friends and relatives. They would sit talk, laugh so much and have tea or coffee. Her main friends I remember were Violet and Ruth. I remember many times we'd go to Violet's or Violet would come over. Many times, we'd go to Ruth's at night, and they'd play cards we call it pasakuaraq. You would call it solitaire, but they'd play like 4 people and see who would finish all their cards first. All the aces go in the center followed by the same suit from aces to kings. Whoever finished first would get a mark by their name. Whoever got 5 marks first would be the winner. They played for hours starting from 7 pm and go on till midnight. Laughing and having so much fun and they would play sitting on the floor. My brother Seymour Jr. and I would follow them and play with their kids, we would play hide and seek. One time I was hiding the adults were taking a break from playing pasakuaraq, my dad was standing by the stove enjoying the heat and he had his legs spread out while standing, I got in front of him and stood like how he was standing and hide there. It took whoever was looking awhile to find me. We would stay there all night. Until about 15 minutes to midnight three blinks of lights shut off meaning it's time to turn off the generator and now get ready for bed. They'd get the coleman light and turn it on. After they finish their game, we'd start walking home. This was one of my favorite memories of Ruth, Bernard and

family. My dad and his aunt Ruth grew up together. Ruth is the younger sister of my dad's mom Helen. Ruth and dad grew up close sometimes they would fight as kids like siblings, and I would hear stories of those sometimes, but they really cared for each other's. I would sometimes follow Emma to her house. Emma is one of Ruth and Bernard's daughters. She is the same age as I am just a few months older. One day we went there after playing out all day. Ruth said there's caribou soup you girls eat. She gave us a bowl and gave us tea. We were sitting on a bench where the table was, and I was going to put sugar in my tea instead I put it in my soup. Ruth burst out laughing and said: "Awe here I'll spill that and give you another bowl". She gave me another bowl and this time I made sure I didn't do the same thing.

Their family made a big impact on a lot of us who lived in Point Hope. Ruth use to sell bread like 50 cent a loaf. They were so good to eat too. Many other families made bread and sold it too. My mother –in-law to be at that time Aggie sold bread, apple pie and the best homemade ice cream. They had a pool hall where men would come and play pool. They also had a little store. I remember going there one time. I really wanted to buy a magic marker. Never seeing one before or owning one. I heard from Maria there is a magic marker you can use to write. It's something different. So, I asked mom I want a quarter to go buy magic marker at Andrew's store (my father-in-law) at that time to be father-in-law. I got brave and went to buy and he was there all by himself, so I thought. I knocked and he answered he asked what I wanted, and I told him I wanted to buy something from his store. We went to the place where he had his store. I pointed at the magic marker, because I didn't know the name and he kept teasing me and points at something different. I kept saying no and finally he points at the magic marker. I said yes. After I paid him, I walked out, and he said wait I turned around and he came and put his arm around me and said I find myself a little girlfriend. I smiled and kept walking out. Well, many years later I got married to his son and my husband now said I was upstairs sick, and I heard my dad say that and I wanted to see who he was talking to, and I saw you.

There was another place too where they had a pool hall, and this was my dad's uncle. He had a little restaurant that sold burgers, they also sold homemade donuts. My husband to be at that time said one time he was playing pool and my dad's uncle made a hint to him and said if I was young, I would go after that girl meaning me. So, I always think that God had this all planned for our marriage. There also was another place that had a pool hall, and this was my mom's brother. They had a little store too. These three places had their business maybe at the same time or a little time after each other's. They were fun places to go to at night. I remember New Years Eve my dad's uncle's place use to be open past midnight. We got to play cards one time while some guys were playing pool. We played dirty eight might have been like 5 or more of us. Boy did we have fun. Our Native people have the best humor of all. Frances, the owner let us continue to play till like 2 am or even

later. Only on new years eve they kept the coffee shop open late and it seems like it was the best time ever. No alcohol involved and so much laughter with a fun game.

I remember we used to play marbles outside whether it be summer or winter. We'd played pots or rings. Pots you'd make a bowl size pot on the ground and draw a line about 12 or more feet away from the pot. Then you would decide how many marbles to put in the pot. You can put as many as you want. Then you'd see who goes first by shooting a marble from the pot to the line closest to the line gets to shoot first, then second, third and so on. Then they shoot a marble towards the pot and try to make it in the pots if it goes in from the line you can win the all the marbles in the pot. If no one wins it after they all get to shoot from the line, they go back to the first person who shot closest to pots from the line and that person would try to make all the marbles. Whoever makes the last marble in the pot wins all the marbles. If you made the marble in the pot from the line you win all the marbles. Then you would start a new game. Ruth and Bernard's kids had a coffee can full of marbles. Make everyone wish they had a lot of marbles. I used to buy 3 marbles for a nickel and never win. I wanted to own a coffee can full of marbles too, but never did.

Life in Point Hope was so quiet, and everyone always lived in harmony. There was hardly any booze and no drugs. I think the drugs like marijuana came to Point Hope in the 70's. We didn't have to lock our doors when we left our houses. Some would tie the outside door with a string, and we'd know the family is not home and we'd leave. It seems like there was no crimes like stealing or no domestic violence. Our days were longer and there was no stress. I would say they really were the best times of our lives. Most of the town went to church on Sunday. The days seem so long and sunshiny days. Peaceful and quiet people visiting each other, you can hear the dogs and kids playing out. Kids would play a lot of outside games like kick the can, Inupiaq baseball and a lot more games. I remember in the summer when the high school teens got back from wherever they were sent to school, they would go to church all dressed up they looked so cool. The guys would go in nice white shirts and nice slacks. Some would wear nice skintight white jeans. The girls would wear skirts or dresses. Boy did they dress good for church. I remember going to church with my grandma Lily every Sunday morning, Sunday at 4pm and on Wednesday night. I would have to sit by her. She taught me how to sit still and if I turn around, she would with her finger to my nose move my head towards the preacher. I learned right away never to do that again. If I had gum, she would take that away from me. I remember Wednesday night Jack and I stuck at church while all the other kids played out on a nice night. It all paid off I became a Christian when I got older, and I learned the songs and hymns by following her to church. My grandma Lily, my mom's mom was always praying when she woke up in the morning, then when she had her first meal and after she's done eating. Every meal and after every meal she'd pray then going to bed was the longest. She was praying one night, and she started laughing, she laughed so pretty and

couldn't stop. At that time, I couldn't understand that, but I knew God touched her. She had a smell on her that I loved. It smelt like burnt wood, but I just loved that smell on her. A lot of kids feared her and said she was mean, to me she was strict she wasn't mean to me. I really loved my aaka Lily, we called her Kinneeveauk's mom. My oldest brother Emmanuel was raised by her. His Inupiaq name was Kinneeveauk that's why we called her that, we followed our oldest sister, Grace who started calling her Kinneeveauk's mom. She was sent to Fairbanks to a home and that's where she passed. When my mom went to pick her up, the ladies working there said they never heard any one pray so much not like her. My aaka even in her state of mind with dementia never forgot to pray. Thank you, Jesus.

We didn't have running water those days and we were content. We would have to get water for drinking, cooking, washing, bathing and washing clothes. I remember going to the other side of the landing field to get water. We would carry water with a tub two of us or three of us would carry and taking turns if there were three of us. Probably most of the town did that, but some had a well-made close to their house. In the winter the men had to get ice with their dog team and later came snow machines. They got the ice from the lagoon or the river. The ice was used for drinking and cooking. They would pile up the ice outside of the houses. We never wasted the ice and we never used it for washing, we always get snow for washing and if we ran out of ice, we make sure we got clean snow and use that for drinking and cooking. We would have a basin for washing our hands and a bucket underneath to spill the dirty water. We would take a bath in the tub all using the same water. My mom would wash clothes by hand and use a washboard. She would hang clothes outside on a homemade clothesline. It was made with two poles on each end and rope tied from pole to pole. She had a 2x4x8 or something like that to keep the rope up and she'd put it in the middle to keep the clothes from touching the ground. In the summer they wouldn't take long to dry, and she'd bring the laundry in and it sure would make the house smell good. Wintertime she would still hang the clothes and they would freeze, then she'd hang them inside to dry. In the house we had rope from one end of the house to the other. Every time we open the door steam would be going outside from the house. We also used honey buckets for the toilet. We would spill it outside in a ditch where our dad dug. He put a 55-gallon barrel and dug it down and put it in so we can spill the honey bucket there. Some used a chamber made from enamel. Especially the elders used them.

Growing up we didn't have many toys. I remember using a big heavy rock for a doll one time, but one time when I got older, I remember my mom letting me order a whole bunch of toys from Sears Roebuck. I ordered a pretend cash register, small vacuum and a lot of other toys. She let me order clothes one time and I ordered for husky kids and man were they too big. I think she returned them. I remember living in Kotzebue and my cousin Sandy had a white bike with pink color stripes. I didn't have one and I used to run alongside her. My

dad might have felt bad for me and said to me one time I'm getting you a bike when I leave for Fairbanks what kind do you want. He went to Fairbanks for National Guard and brought home a nice boy's bike. My dad probably didn't know the difference between a girl's bike or boy's bike. It was a copper-colored bike, and it was so cool. I used it in Kotzebue. One time I went to see a robin nest I found riding my bikes. I put the bikes down and didn't know there were boys hiding waiting for the mother robin to come back I remember praying God let that nest still be there or something like that. The boys got up and startle me one of them took my bike and ran off with it. I ran home and told my parents, and my dad went out and ran after them hollering at them. The kid threw my bike and ran off. Dad got my bike back. People always told me my dad was a fast runner. When he was young, he ran with the reindeer. He had big calves and when he sat on the floor with his legs touching the floor his feet couldn't touch the floor. We lived at Kotzebue in the summer the late 60's to early 70's my dad worked for the hotel where the tourist stayed. He was one of the maintenance men. My mom worked at a lot of different places like the hotel she made certificates for the tourist. She worked at Rotman Store once, she baby sat for a single mom and the one thing we all did to earn money was Inupiaq Dancing for the tourist. My dad carved and the tourist would watch him. There was this other guy that did that too his name was Charlie.

We would entertain tourist from all over the world and states. We would start the night with blanket toss. They would let us younger ones get on it and toss us up the sky like two stories high or something like. The blanket toss was made from bearded seal skin. I would go on the blanket toss and twirl coming down. It was fun when you were used to doing it every night. Then they would go in the building and Inupiaq dance for the tourist. They would start out by motion dance. Motion dance is a dance that can tell a story or just a fun dance. Then once all the dancers did their dance, they would do a common dance and invite everyone to dance. The ladies bend their knees to the beat of the drums, and they move one side arm to the front then to the back like swimming. Those days they had the best drums and they always beat the drums in harmony. They sounded so good. The men stomp their feet to the beat of the drum and move their arms from side to side. Like showing strength and flexing. Then after their done they would put out tables and start laying their artwork and sell them. We would get paid by every time we attend the dance and blanket toss. My dad built a sod house for the tourist to go in and show them how they use to live and how they were built. My dad also made a cage big enough for two reindeers to live in. The size was big as a one-bedroom house. It had a door that you can latch from the outside. My parents use to let me go in there and feed the reindeers after showing me how safe it is. I was too scared to go in by myself so I would get willows and feed them through the holes of the cage. They would eat right out of my hands. Then when I got brave, I went in one time and fed them. Dad said to make sure and put the latch back on. My grandparents asked my brother Seymour and I to fill a plastic bag full of moss and bring it to my grandparents

and we would get paid 50 cent a bag. One time I filled it more than half and they paid me 50 cents. Next time I didn't really want to pick leaves and I knew I wasn't doing a good job, but that laziness feeling just really got to me. I put in less than half and my grandpa laughed and said nope you need to put more in there. So, I went and put in little more and he said OK that's good and he gave me my 50 cents. It was always good to go over to my grandparent's place even I didn't say anything to them. It was just how we were we never really had a conversation, just sat and watched if they offer you something you took it. If they asked you a question you answered. My grandparents worked with a well-known tourist company, and they traveled many places. They even act in the movie with a well-known actor. Yet my grandparents were humble as can be. I remember traveling with them from Fairbanks to Anchor Point in a car to perform our native dance and to blanket toss. Someone drove us there I can't remember if it was my Aunt Mae or Aunt Mary. Mary might have driven from Fairbanks, and we picked up Mae from Anchorage and then drove to Anchor Point. The weather was getting a little cold so it might have been in the fall. We got into Anchor Point late and straight to where we had to perform it was a little bar. It had a stage and we started dancing on the stage. I didn't know the motions and they told me to copy so I did, and it turned out ok, so I thought. The crowd clapped and cheered when we were done. It was time to go to bed and I went to the room I was to sleep on. It had two twin beds very small room just enough room for the beds. I couldn't sleep and laid there. Later on, I heard my grandpa saying to my grandma "please just one more" he kept repeating it. He wanted to drink one more can of beer. Earlier he had been sitting by the counter and drinking beer. My grandma didn't give in to his pleading for another beer. She kept answering "no time to go to bed" in our Inupiaq language. My aunts didn't come to the room until late I don't know what time I had fallen asleep before they came in. the next day we went to perform on the blanket toss. There were a lot of people that pulled the blanket toss, and they were all white people and we were the only Inupiaqs. I got on the blanket toss because my grandpa made me get on. I got on usually I do a good job and land on my feet but this time it felt different I didn't land on my feet. I think it was because seeing all these white people pulling and I had no confidence in myself. Later, that day we went to the store, and they gave me money to buy what I wanted. So, I bought me some big mouth candy. Wow this was my first time ever to see one like that and I really wanted to taste it. I bought two of the big mouth candy and something else I don't really remember. I remember later that night before I went to bed, I tried one and I laid there on the bed sucking on it and finally when I reached the center it got a little soft and I was able to bite on it and then wow there was gum. The tastiest gum I ever tried. I don't remember our ride back to Fairbanks all I remember just a little bit of our ride there and the things that we did in Anchor Point. This all might have been somewhere around 1967 or later. Going to Anchor Point was one trip I never forgot. I still can remember some parts of it, and it never left me. Although I never really talked to my grandparents

and my aunties, I got to be with them and got to know them more. My grandma was very beautiful and so my aunties were very beautiful. My dad had a big family, and they were all handsome and beautiful. My dad's biological dad died January 1, 1958. His name was Bob and was sent to Seattle Hospital and when he died, they didn't send his body home he was buried in Seattle. Later, my grandma Helen remarried Chester Seveck I don't know what year. My aaka Helen and Seveck are the ones that did all the tourist work.

January in Point Hope use to be very cold the ice would be frozen on the ice. This is the time of year my dad would be going on the ice to hunt seals. We would be going to school very cold, and some would wake up to frozen wash water in the basin and thaw it out with their hands. It's dark this time of the year. Wake up to dark and run to school in the dark and no transportation. No one had vehicles to ride to school. It would be a little dark after school. I remember running home from school when it was dark and no streetlights. It was scary so dark can't see but we always made it to the store or home.

February was like January cold and maybe colder like some days minus 60 below. This time of the year they would hunt seals and the little fish cods. March was also a cold month. It's the time of getting ready for whaling. The men will sharpen their knives for cutting the whale. They would renew their paddles by shaving the wood. It's a lot of work preparing for whale season. The woman would make new warm parkas and maklaks. This is the month they pray for the whaling hunters and tools. Captains and their wives go to the church and gather for a service called Rogation. The men will bring something they use to hunt whales with. Like they will bring their skin boat in the church and the rest will bring a paddle, spear, harpoon or anything that they will use to hunt. They still do that today.

We had long and slow days, peaceful and quiet. Our people were always respectful majority of the time. Our people laughed a lot they loved to make jokes. Never a serious moment seems like it.

Later in the 70's I use to miss those days when we were just getting into new ways of living. I didn't want to move on, but we had no choice people change, situations change and a lot of it was money changed our people. Too much money was floating around people started working on the slope and started bringing in booze from all directions. There were jobs from relocating the town and building new homes. What a cultural shock it felt like we were numb and getting cold on the inside. Times change, people change, had to hold on to sanity.

April was a lot of snow and getting a little warmer, we had a lot of stormy days, and nothing stopped us from going to school. We all made it to school windy, raining or stormy. Some days couldn't even see in front of us because of the blowing snow. This month they would be going out whale hunting as soon as a man that's been hunting reports there's a whale or beluga spotted. Then that's the time they go out whaling. This is the beginning of exciting days for the people of Point Hope all waiting and praying for a whale to be caught. When a captain and his

crew catch the first whale everyone is so happy. They bring in the whale's flipper and everyone goes to the family home. They ring the church bell. We would run to the church bell to see who caught a whale. Sometimes during school when someone catches a whale, we were not able to go there if the teacher says no. Sometimes when we are able to go see who caught a whale, we would have to return to school promptly. People will be crying happy tears and rejoice. One of the happiest days never fail and will be the same for every crew that catches a whale. It is very much the same today. They still gather by the church bell when someone catches a whale. The joy of catching a whale will never end. In May the crews are still hunting. During the whale hunting season, they hunt ducks, seals, belugas, small crabs and the one they really want is the whales. They just love the small and round whale. It is so tender and delicious to eat. June is the time they start cleaning up and put away the whaling stuff. They start getting ready for the whaling feast. On the second Sunday of the month of June is usually the 1st day of the whaling feast.They celebrate whaling feast for three days. The first day of the feast the men and the captain who caught a whale race with their skin boats from the beach to the place they set up for the first day of the feast. There they will serve a little of the fermented whale, donuts, coffee, tea and cake. At night they come to church and sing, give testimonies. Some ladies stay home and prepare for the next two days. They finish up their parkas, maklaks or make inupiaq ice cream. The second day they celebrate on the celebration place. Where it's been set up for years.

Two clans left in Point Hope one qaqmaktuuk and ungisiksiqaq. They give out more of the fermented whale and the captain and wife pass out flippers of the whale to each person they would like to give. The captain and his wife are dressed in their best regalia. Also the crew are most of the people are dressed so nice in their new parka's and new maklaks.They inupiaq dance and do they blanket toss. Last day they go early in the morning and serve breakfast and cook all the parts of the whale. They dance and blanket toss after cooking all the parts. Then they go to the gym and inupiaq dance and give out frozen maktak and meat. They always pray from the starting of the feast and the ending they pray also. After whaling feast, they start hunting bearded seals and walrus. July, they start going boating on the coast to pick murre eggs. They hunt caribous and the ladies start to hang dry bearded seals and make seal oil. Towards the end of July, it starts getting dark. Point Hope usually in May 24 hour daylight starts and starts getting dark in July. That month they continue to hunt caribou and the end of July they start using net to catch fish. Sometimes they start as early in last part of June. August is the time to pick berries the salmon berries and blue berries. They continue in September. When we were growing up in the mid 60's we use to all work as soon as you turn 12 when you get your social security you can start working. The big boat called North Star use to come in August and bring food and all that for the store. The people of Point Hope use to work by carrying the food and all that from the barges to the shore. They all get paid. Men and women working day

and night. Seems like the whole town would be out by the beach day and night or after school the kids would be there. It was fun being out there at night they would put lights and if you weren't working, we'd sit out there watching the people or we'd be walking around there and just enjoy talking telling stories. We could hear the ladies laughing and they would have the loudest laugh. I remember one time my classmate Alice and I were there, and she said to me let's call each other's arumaluk. There was these two ladies that called one another that. So we started calling one another arumaluk that night. Arumaluk meant like same or twin like. She wanted to be like these two ladies that called each others that.

About October or earlier they would go to the river Kukpaq River and set nets or ice fish for grayling. They would also catch some rainbow trout. They would keep doing this sometimes till December. The grayling fish taste so good with seal oil. We all love that time of the year so we can eat frozen grayling and seal oil. Yummy the best ever.

Ephesians 2: 8-9 For by grace are ye saved through faith; and that not of yourselves: it is the gift of God: 9 Not of works, lest any man should boast.

When my life changed was in August of 1994. I always wanted to be a Christian wife since I was young. I always dream of being a Christian wife. It took 20 years to finally come to realize I need to do it now. I decided to follow Jesus. It took a while, but I know the Lord was working on me. I remember our trip in 1991 or 1992 to Vegas there was 8 of us. We were there for 2 weeks so we decided to take a road trip our relatives friends rented a van and we went with them from Las Vegas to Flagstaff. We each got our own room. We were so tired and we just laid on the bed turn the TV on. Didn't know what to watch and there it was on a Christian program we thought it was a regular news. We didn't know it was a Christian news. There was a guy saying they have a lady who experienced life and death situation. She said she died and was going towards hell it was getting hot and smelly. She can hear people hollering she was getting closer and closer. Then suddenly, she went back to her body. Here she said she worked with elderly people and care for them. She was a Sunday school teacher but didn't know why she was going to hell. I was thinking she sounded better than I am so if she is going to hell I must be too. It got to where I wanted to watch this and find out why she was going to hell. So, the guy was saying she was doing all this on her own by works. She didn't accept Jesus as her Savior. So, I remembered how the prayer this guy was saying he said if you wanted to except Jesus as your Lord and Savior repeat after me. I always remembered the prayer. I used to go to the bathroom and pray, still do the same thing over and over drinking and never change. Finally, I was crying and like I was praying to

Jesus like he was right in front of me. I was saying it from my heart and not from my mouth.

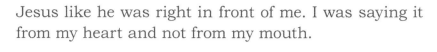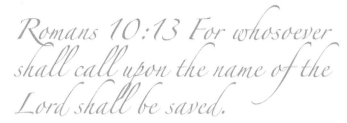

Romans 10:13 For whosoever shall call upon the name of the Lord shall be saved.

In August 1994 I went to my neighbors across the street my cousin invited me to her brother's place for singsperation. My cousin and I were working at the clinic and when on breaks cigarette break, we would talk of the Lord. That's when she invited me to her brother's place. We were singing a few of us and the pastor of the church he and his wife were there also. When it was time to end the pastor said let's pray before we go home. So, we went in a circle and held hands and prayed. I prayed from my whole heart, I prayed and ask God to help me to quit drinking. I didn't care if anyone heard me, I prayed from my heart. I was so happy, and I knew something happened.

I went home and the next day or, so I was so happy washing dishes singing in my mind "I have decided to follow Jesus". I couldn't wait for Sunday I wanted to go to church. I was going to a bible based believing church even my dad was a minister of another church I wanted to go to this other church. I always remember this one lady when I was little and had to follow my aaka (grandma) Lily to church, she went to this other church and when 4pm Sunday service came she'd come and give her testimony. Four o'clock service was for singing and testimony at the church I grew up. I just knew going there would help me.

I was so different from the inside like I was seeing things so different. One day I was outside, and it was winter the sun was out, I looked at the snow it looked so beautiful like I can see diamonds sparkling all over. I never ever seen it like that before, I never really admired it like I did that day. God was showing me differently how I saw things.

I started going to church and they accepted me. There was a pastor from another village his wife and children. I learned a lot from the pastor. I was so amazed how the word of God was alive. The bible became so real to me like never before. I believed it when I heard it and when I read it. I would be so happy reading or hearing it. I would cry or just raise my hands. I started sharing my testimony or scriptures to the church on Sunday evening. The pastor and his wife took us to another village for Easter once and I think that was when I started sharing my testimony to a crowd other than the church.

When the pastor and his family left and moved, we were without a pastor, the board members ran the church they did so good. It wasn't new to them they had done it before. We had a lady that mentored us her name was Esther. She was the best mentor we could ever asked for. A whole bunch of us got saved that year. Can you imagine a whole bunch of us wanting to learn, wanting to be set free. We were so hungry all just learning how to walk with the Lord. We would sing and praise God, cry and praying all the time. Sunday night and Wednesday nights were the nights for singing and

testimony. This is how I grew in the spirit. We learned how to share with the power of the Holy Spirit.

The Lord worked in me in so many ways to heal my broken spirit. I wanted to please my God as truthful as I can. He started working in me through ways I never experienced before. I was a health aide at the time. I had been working at the clinic maybe since 1986 could be earlier. Going back before I got saved in 1991, we had loss our son Ebrulik Bobby he was only four and was going to turn five the next month. That day was the hardest day of my life the pain was so great, it was like a knife was in my chest. That morning we got up my husband Ira and me. I got Ebrulik dressed, and he said to me I don't want to go to school. Can I stay home? I said you need to go to school no one to watch you, but after school your uncle Kinneeveauk will be here to watch you. He ended up going to school. In a way I'm glad he did go to school. He got to see his siblings for the last time that day. My brother was there for him after school. My brother told me what he said to him that day I'm going to Jesus today. I am sitting here at the airport waiting to board a plane when I got a call from one of the ladies where I worked "Martha, they want you to stay here your son been hit with a car. A broken leg they are bringing him here". My heart sank my baby, my son my 4-year-old. I had escorted a baby this morning to Kotzebue from my hometown Point Hope. The next call came few minutes later something about they want you to go home. My question did he not make it? I didn't know I called the clinic in Point Hope no one told me what had happened they couldn't tell me. Then Ethel got the phone and told me he didn't make it. The lady where I worked asked if I wanted someone to follow me to go home on the plane, I said yes. I kept crying more and more as we got closer to Point Hope. I saw my husband and my first reaction I wanted to hug him so bad, but people got in the way to hug me my parents weren't there. I barely can remember every detail with who or how we got to my mom's place someone took us from the airport to my mom's. My dad met me at the door, and we hugged and cried. My mom was sitting by the table crying so loud and she didn't even respond to me. She cried for so many hours just sitting there crying. My mom was so close to our son. She would baby him and wanted the best for him. She was so heart broken for our son. I never got to talk to my mom that day. She was in her own world crying nothing we did or say couldn't stop her from crying. I never seen my mom cry so much. We finally went home to our kids. Someone had been there all day making sure they ate. We went to the clinic to see my son I wanted to hold him so bad. I saw his body just lying there it wasn't even my son just a empty shell no life. Where was the breathing soul that I knew. His personality, his smartness, his loving and caring soul that I knew where did it go? My son had gotten runned over by a bus. Life was so different few days later I was sitting on the couch all alone and I was crying I thought I should just kill myself. I had my eyes closed then open my eyes right in front of me was a knife. I don't remember if it was there or how it got there. Then all sudden I thought no way am I going to kill myself. I got mad at the devil. There was a bible next to me and

I got it and opened it I saw a scripture and God was speaking to me. I don't remember the scripture, but I wish I did. I felt so happy that God was speaking to me. Our son was so smart and obedient. He was our baby and we had so much plans for him. He learned how to spell his name, sing the ABC's and count to 10 when he was 1 years old. People got tickled over him spelling his name, because he would say E-b-r-me-l-i-k. There was this guy every time he saw our son he'd ask him to spell his name, a lot of people did that, but this guy never missed and always laugh a little cause he thought it was so cute. He was the cutest ever. Never think we'd lose him at an early age. It was the saddest day ever for us. When we had funeral for him his classmates' little kids so cute as can be all went to the funeral with their teacher and they each carried a flower. The church was so full standing room only and my husband said some standing outside. The memory of it all is painful, but yet the people there made it so loving. Well one night I was lying in bed must have been two months before he died or somewhere around there. I woke up to some presence like someone was watching us. I looked at our door and it was opened halfway. Then at the corner of the opening I saw an all-white dressed person like just passed by. I wasn't scared and was thinking I'm not going to scared of anyone walking in our house. I woke up Ira and hollered hey who's there? I got up to check the rooms and went to check the storm shed and no one was there. We didn't have a landline phone at that time, so I went on our VHF and got a hold of our family next door. My sister answered and I asked her if anyone came here, she said she didn't think so. Still today I don't know what it was and later thought it might be an angel of death or I don't know.

Fast forward to 1994 when I got saved, I had been carrying the hurt and not letting my son go, because it would make me feel like I didn't love him. One day or night I was worshipping God in church. I had been worshipping him from my heart and started crying and praising God deep from my heart. While I was worshipping the Lord, he said to me I have your son. I started crying even more. I gave my son back to God in the spirit I let go of my son. I felt and I knew something left and I felt lighter. I was so honored that God wanted my son. He was my gift from God, and I gave him back. God allowed it to happen for his glory. When I was in the world there was no hope, but with God, he gave me hope to see my son again. Hallelujah there is coming a day I'll get to see Jesus first and I'll get to see my son. I don't ever want to miss that day.

So many different things started to happen seem like God was tickling me a little baby. We are like newborn babies in Christ and the Lord enjoys it when we are hungry for the word, he makes sure we get filled. I was so broken before I accepted Jesus into my life. So many tragic things happened in my life. So many deaths happened to my family. I remember one time I went to a gathering in a convocation there was a whole bunch of us that went. We had been in the service and at the ending the pastor invited us to come up for prayer. I think Greg was preaching that night. So, I went up for prayers I always love to get prayed for when it was altar

call. I think I went up for every altar call no matter where I went to church. I always went up for prayers even if the altar call didn't pertain to me. It was just me I wanted to be pure and close to God. I believed that he can do miracles and everything that we asked by faith. The lady that always use to come to testimony time at church when I was little made me believe that God can do all that. I went up for prayers and they prayed over me I fell and laid there crying I don't know how long I was just crying and suddenly in my mind I thought of my younger four siblings that died in a fire when I was 8 years old. God reminded me of that. My sister Helen next to me my brother Bobby, sister Lisa and youngest sister Dolly. I thought of them, and I knew why I had been crying so hard. I had been carrying the hurt for so long that I didn't know it and the Lord reminded me and I had to be healed. That cry for them was from deep inside me and I cried for so long and they let me be. A lot of people were on the floor too. Some were laughing, crying, some quiet and some praying. When I was done I got up and my whole being felt so light. I felt so happy from deep within. Things like God tickling started to happen. Scriptures like 7:38 became so real to me.

John 7: 38 He that believeth on me, as the scripture hath said, out of his belly shall flow rivers of living water.

One day my husband and I got into argument. I was so hurt that I didn't stand strong and keep my mouth shut. I went to my mom's house to make a phone call. My parents were in Anchorage no one was at the house. I made a call to this well known Christian television program I always called them when I needed prayers when I couldn't call Esther. I called and a guy answered. I told him I am a Christian and I was just had an argument with my husband. I told him I needed to be prayed for. He asked, "Have you been baptized with the evidence of speaking in tongues?" I said no, "he asked do you want it?" I said, I guess. Then he prayed for me I can't remember what he said. I was holding a bible on my right hand and the phone on my left hand, and I was crying and praying. Then he said speak it now. I said I didn't know how. He said speak it. He wouldn't stop saying that to me, so I just mumbled. He wanted me to open my mouth by faith. He said OK now when we hang up read the whole chapter of John 15. So, when we hang up, I sat on the couch and started reading John 15. I was just praising God and shouting hallelujah. It was Jesus, he was preaching to me. So anointed he is, just so anointed. I didn't see Jesus preaching but I knew in my heart it was him, I was crying and praising God. The reading was so real life like, and I understood every word of it. I was imaging everything that I was reading. That day I was on call it must have been a weekend and I know it was at night. I was a health aide, and someone called so I had to go to the clinic. I got there and was trying my best to help the patient. Then the lady with her started hollering at me. Later on, the patient got good, and I was driving home, and I

was like Lord I try my best to help people and never get appreciated. I said get me out of this job. I was having a pity party. Then I went home all the lights were out. My heart sank my husband and I never got to make up. I went to straight to the bedroom. My husband slept on the couch. I turned the TV on to a well known Christian channel. When I turned it on there was a guy preaching on John 15 hallelujah! Wow I was so amazed John 15 and God's timing a divine appointment. I was so blessed I started praising God sitting on the foot side of the bed. I started feeling like a tingling feeling on my arms. Then from my belly a warm water feeling, something alive was moving. It was going up and up towards my mouth. It felt like a butterfly or something. God is so real and the experience I had that night is so unexplainable. It was like electricity, but no pain. I can't explain it, but I loved it. I was just in so much awe, I don't know how long I was worshipping, and I don't remember if it was the same guy. He said you sitting there, ya you hold on to your job. I cried and was so happy. God of the universe so big and so awesome would even make a mere person feel so special. I know if he can do that for me, he can do that for all. After that day I didn't care where I was, I was praising God and letting all who was with me know that God can save them as he did for me. The Father had made himself so real to me. I know that there is nothing on earth no alcohol, no drug, no man nothing can compare to the feeling of how God can make you feel. Nothing can compare to how he loves you. When you are humble to him when you pray, he hears you. When you want him more than anything else he hears you. God is God, no one like him that wants you to make him first in your life. Hallelujah!

There were times more than once before this happened to me. We had a red ford explorer, after the morning service church I would go for a ride with my daughters or with one of my friends. We would go towards the seven-mile road, and I would drive further off the seven-mile road where there was dirt road. It was a rough road, where people with four-wheelers and snowmachines drove. I would drive that way and never realize that even when I take my feet off the gas or press on my brakes that nothing would happen. It would keep going the same no matter what I do. If it was bumpy the ride would be smooth all the way. I later heard a testimony from someone in Anchorage said they did that when after being so filled in the spirit and went for ride. That's when it clicked, I have experience that before so many times, because I have been do filled, I never notice it. All that mattered to me that time I was touched, and the joy of the Lord was on me. I would be just talking and laughing after church and driving. It was angels driving and carrying the car seems like. Hallelujah!

Psalm 50:15 And call upon me in the day of trouble: I will deliver thee, and thou shall glorify me.

There was a lot that was in me that God needed to work on. He knows what I'm holding on to and what need to leave. When he delivered me from alcohol, he instantly delivered me, but one thing I couldn't stop smoking I tried but failed so many times. Even before I got saved, I was trying to quit. So, after I got saved, I kept asking for prayers to quit smoking. I prayed and asked God to help me quit. One night I was in evening service can't remember if it was Sunday night or Wednesday night, I was so filled so light and happy. After church I went home, I started hiding smoking, so I went to the one storm shed where the double door was. I lit a cigarette and there I felt the Lord looking right at me in front of me. The Holy Spirit left from my presence, and I went in the living room and got on my knees right by the couch. I prayed and cried Lord you got to help me quit I can't quit on my own. My husband and I went to Anchorage I can't remember what it was for. I couldn't wait to go to church where we would go when we go to Anchorage. I knew something good was going to happen. I thought my husband was going to give himself to the Lord. I remember it was the week before Halloween on a Wednesday 1995 we went to church. When we got there, they were praising God and worshipping him. I just got right into worshipping, and I had a pack of Marlboro lights in my pocket. So, we were praising and suddenly everyone got quiet. Then this lady stood up and said there's someone here that has a habit, and the Lord is saying there's no time to be playing around. You with that habit stop it. She said it so clear and with authority with the power of the Holy Spirit. I knew it was me. I surrendered and lifted my hands up I was crying. I was thinking I hope they anoint people with oil I want to be prayed for. Then when the preacher got up to speak, he said we're going to do something different for those of you that need prayers come up and make a line we will anoint you will oil and pray for you. Hallelujah! Usually at the end of the service they ask people to come up for prayers, but this time they did it in the beginning. I went in line and was so happy. It was my turn, and I went up to be prayed for. I asked the Lord to deliver me from cigarette smoking. When the service was over, we went in our little black car, at the time I really didn't know names of the cars, cars were cars, trucks were trucks. It was little and black. We always lit a cigarette after church. My husband lit his and I didn't I looked at him and I couldn't smell the cigarette smell. It was like I was in a bubble; something was covering me. Only way I was able to smell the smoke was if I took a deep sniff from my nose, but even if I took a deep sniff to smell I smelt only a little of it. I was protected and God proved that this was him moving in me. I was so happy in my mind I was praising God hallelujah. I didn't tell Ira about it until I told my testimony. We went to the room we were at and I threw my carton of Marlboro lights, crushed them and threw them away, but I kept the one pack in my pocket just in case if I crave in the morning, because in the morning is when I really craved for a cigarette. The next morning, I didn't crave hallelujah! Praise the Lord I was delivered. I never craved for a cigarette again. I got tempted, but I never smoked again. I used to dream that I was smoking a cigarette and felt bad that I started smoking again. Then sometimes I'd dream I'd start drinking again. I

would really feel so bad and wake up so happy that it was only a dream. One time we went to church I won't name the place. They were having communion, we had communion with them. It was my turn for them to serve me the wine, and I gave them my bread, and they dipped it in the wine gave it to me. I got a buzz as I was walking to where I was sitting. I got that buzz I once knew before I had quit drinking. I haven't had a drink since 1994 and that little dipping of the bread got me high. I sat there and quickly that down feeling like how when we were sobering up came. I felt that darkness of sobering up, I was like thank you Jesus for reminding me where I came from. I never want to ever turn back to alcohol. Hallelujah!

One night I went to bed and Ira was next to me. Like the Lord was talking to me and thoughts were coming I can't remember what it was I remembered a little. He was saying something like go to your old church and speak. He said I'd be like Sarah and I was like have a baby in an old age like Sarah? Then I felt the Spirit of God in my belly was so strong, and I wanted to laugh so loud, and I didn't want to wake my husband up, so I got up to the living room and laughed oh the joy of the Lord was so strong. Like a bubble coming out of my mouth. I called my mentor and told Esther. I can't remember what we said, but it was late, and we said good night. That was so silly that I said that and how I said it. Maybe to me I will be like Sarah in the spirit. I don't know still today, but one day it'll all be revealed. The bubble feeling is so hard to explain, but the joy of laughter is so deep and can't keep it in. God showed up in his awesome, most powerful way. Nothing in this earth can give you joy as much as Father God can. I love him so much now and even more than ever.

I used to go pray with this one lady when she needed prayer and one night while I was praying for her, I felt a little heat like warm water just about maybe a grape size around the right side of my belly. I didn't say anything to her. I startled then it went away. That's when the Lord showed me, I can be praying for someone, and he can be working on me. That spot where I felt that warm like water feeling is where I have a scar from removing gall stones and they made a long cut to my appendix, it was a choice they gave me. To have my appendix removed same time. I was so blessed that God showed me how when we fervently pray for someone how he can touch us too. This feeling was like warm water or electricity again and hard to explain. God healed me in that area while I was praying for someone.

When we were without a pastor, we use to share testimonies, share a song this really helped me to walk with the Lord and to be true to him, to walk and do the word, because people heard me, and I just wanted to be a true witness to the Lord. It also sharpened my tools to share the word. We were always praying, each one of us loudly. We cried a lot; the ladies had a soft heart. When we cried it wasn't like we did something wrong and we had regretted it, maybe sometimes it was, but when we got so filled and he touch our hearts we just cried. The Lord's presence was so strong and beautiful. One time the ladies were praying and suddenly like a

wind blew on us as we were praying holding hands in a circle. God did so much for us to show his glory. We all swayed to one direction. Hallelujah!

Later, we got a pastor who had a family. He asked whoever wants to share a word on Wednesday night can volunteer. I don't know how many before me shared. Then one day I volunteered, and I fasted that day and prayed. I shared out of your belly shall flow rivers of living water. I shared my testimony. There was the same lady who I would go pray with she told me that night when I shared, she never felt like anything like this before. She said she gave every part of her body to the Lord, she gave her hands, her legs, her face, her tongue, every part even her all her organs and her muscles, and she got so happy she just wanted to laugh.

There was a time the Lord showed me how powerful our words were. So, when I got filled as we are worshipping in church, I use to feel like a big megaphone was in my mouth. Like my praises were going out so strong as I'm singing like so powerful. I imagine as I'm singing it goes out of my mouth and it's does something in the spirit realm that I can't see. It goes out like a warfare and breaking curses. I believe when we enter the spirit realm as we are worshipping, we go into battle and the Lord does it for us. When we are in tune with the Lord. When our hearts are right with the Lord. When we get out of our flesh there is a level of praise we can enter in and that is the spiritual realm. Most of the time we don't even get out of our flesh to worship. Sometimes as we are just entering in, and someone stops the worship. Just when we entered in when God himself wants to say something someone stops the worship. I felt that so many times before. God wants us to worship in spirit and in truth. Hallelujah and thank you Jesus. Let us learn to worship you in spirit and truth and not hinder you.

Dreams started to happen I dreamt I was in a little house and people were just praising God and so happy. When I walked in, I felt the wave of God I couldn't balance standing there. When it was over people were walking out and this lady that I had been mad at for being angry at my adult kids. I was thinking I'm not going to ever talk to her again or something like that. She passed by me, and I asked her did you feel it too? She passed by me saying no I didn't feel anything, she was mad. When I woke up it was so strong in my memories. The Lord had showed me when we don't love and forgive people like we should we put a barrier in the spirit, and they can't receive. So, when I realized that I repented and said forgive me Lord. I choose to love and forgive her.

For a long time, I'd pray for Ira's salvation one night I dreamt there was a hand in the sky a hand so real, but I can see through it. It was transparent. I was so in awe praising God then Ira who was next to me fell on his knees and was crying asking God to forgive him. God who is mighty all mighty can do anything with his mighty hand can save and nothing can stop him.

Daniel 1:17 As for these four children, God gave them

knowledge and skill in all learning and wisdom: and Daniel had understanding in all visions and dreams.

Acts 2:17 And it shall come to pass in the last days, saith God, I will pour out of my Spirit upon all flesh: and your sons and daughters shall prophesy, and your young men shall see visions, and your men shall dream dreams:

One night I dreamt I was in a boat driving in the sky. I was like I'm driving a boat, and I don't even know how to drive a boat. There was a well-known evangelist in front he was leading, and I was driving. We had come from other side of the lower 48 states. We went over 48 states, and it looked so green and blue. Just beautiful and the color and everything was so real. So, we passed and went over Alaska same thing blue and green colors. I can see every detail like the trees the rivers. The trees so green, the rivers so blue. We went to Russia and fear came over me and I wanted to see how close Russia was from Alaska I looked around and saw it was so close. I saw a lady walking in Russia, then looked up front and the evangelist had fallen and was hanging down and holding on to the rope. I was going to help him get up, but thought he is strong he can make it back up to the boat. He got up and when he got up there were three men in the boat up front with him. That night the dream I dreamt seem so real and I was wondering what the interpretation of the dream is. I told my friend the dream and she said whenever your dreaming of a vehicle of any kind it means the ministry. After that I got the meaning of the dream. It meant I was driving meaning when we as prayer warriors praying, we pray for the pastors and all that are taking the word we are taking them places. The beautiful trees are the people, they make the people beautiful they come alive. Green is the color of life. Blue is the color of the Holy Spirit, they make the people come to life with the power of the Holy Spirit. Before the Lord we were dead in our sins so ugly God couldn't see us, but when we become saved, he can see us, he sees us covered with the blood of Jesus. Remember in my dream fear came over me and I was looking how close Russia was from Alaska? It's when we start looking at our situation and take our eyes off God chaos starts happening. I took my eyes off God and the person in front got weak and fell off the ministry, but he was still holding on to God. He was strong in the Lord, and I had faith he'd get back in the ministry safely. He did get back in and when he

did the three men up front that got in with him were the Father, Son and Holy Spirit. Hallelujah!

There was a time when one of my sisters was in the hospital. She had a stoke and for while it was like a roller coaster ride. The doctors would let us go see her and said she wouldn't make it so we would go to the hospital. It was going on for awhile and I was getting very emotional so one morning on the way to work I was crying and praying I was saying God if you're going to take my sister you can take her, but all I'm asking and wanting to know if she's saved. I can't remember if it was that night or when it was I dreamt about my sister. In my dream she was about 12 years old, but she looked old and wrinkle. She looked so ugly, and she was dead laying on a bed. She was laying on a small wooden bed. Then while I was looking at her suddenly, she came alive she was breathing and as soon as she was breathing, she looked so beautiful. She really looked so beautiful. That was my sister I knew. She was still laying on the bed and I didn't want to look at her lower part of her body, because I knew she was naked. I had to look and when I did her nakedness looked so pure and innocent. There was no shame in looking at her. She got up and she had little pair of socks blue and white striped socks. They were so tiny for her. She couldn't put them on. When I woke up I knew what it meant. Father God heard my prayer he had let me know she was saved. Before the Lord she was so ugly and dead. That's how we are when we are sinners. When we accept the gift of life from God, we become alive and so beautiful. She had small socks she was trying to put on it was like she had gotten saved and there was no one to disciple her. When we come to the Father, we become so beautiful and there is no more shame. Thank you Jesus hallelujah! I was so happy my sister was saved. I would go see my sister and even in her state she'd want me to pray with her and worship with her. She always gets so happy to worship and praise God. She was hungry and wanted to hear the word of God. It was a joy to just sit and pray with her she would get so happy and shout hallelujah or amen. I had that little time to worship with my sister. I can't remember how long she lived, but it was a while. She died later and when she did, I knew in my heart where she went. Father God was so faithful he let me know she got saved. My God is so good. The best ever Abba Father, Jehovah Jireh, Elilohim, mighty one, Prince of peace hallelujah. He is the only true God.

There was a time I had a vision. This time before going to church I knew I would receive, I wanted to hear from God I was tired of going to church and not hearing from God. This time I said I'm not going to get distracted. I want to hear and I'm going to enter into God's presence. The worship leader was leading us, and I don't know how long we were worshipping. Then I had a vision of two white flags and the corner of the flags were changing to checkered. I didn't know what it meant. So, I prayed then one night I was going to bed and the Lord said go check on the computer and look up what the flags mean. That morning I went to the computer and went on the internet. I didn't know what to look for then the thought Nascar came to me. I knew it had to be the Lord who

told me to look up Nascar. I googled Nascar what does the flags mean. Went there and then saw that the white flag means one more lap. Ohhhh God you saying we are on the last mile of the way? I looked up black and white checkered means race has ended. God says we are on the last of the days and those days are the hardest. When you're in a race and you're on the last lap you really focus and you're sweating you really want to win. You can't mess up. It's like walking with the Lord the last mile is the hardest Satan is trying his best to stop you. He puts obstacle in the way, but you must stay focus, keep looking straight ahead, don't turn to the right or left. Look at Jesus, he will keep you on the right track. Our victory, our race is almost over. The flags starting to get checkered black and white means our race is almost ended. Hallelujah! Thank you, Jesus! One other time I had bought me a fork bracelet. I always wanted a ring, or some jewelry made of fork. I found a bracelet and I bought it. I was worshipping with my whole heart and then I kept seeing a swastika on my wrist and it never went away. So, when church was almost over, I thought ohhhh I bought a fork jewelry. So, I went home and looked at it sure enough it had a shape of a swastika, so I prayed and ask the Lord to forgive me and remove any curse over me and I threw it away. God always show you things and sometimes it seems it's your own thoughts, but when you keep your eye on him, he will reveal to you what he wants to show you. Hallelujah! Thank you, Jesus. Another time I was worshipping in church and while I was worshipping, I saw a beautiful, strong arm and hands. It was so beautiful and handsome. I really wanted that arm, like I lusted over it. It was so lovable, then I realized that it was Jesus' arm and I needed to really want him and not to lust any man like that. We must love Jesus like no other man. Love God like no other man. Keep looking for our soon coming King, our one and only faithful husband. He is coming for his pure bride. Yes, and amen! Hallelujah!

Isaiah 58:6 Is not this the fast I have chosen? to loose the bands of wickedness, to undo the heavy burdens, and to let the oppressed go free, and that ye break every yoke?

One time I know I needed to fast and pray. I asked my husband if I can get a hotel. If I were to fast and pray at home, I wouldn't pray I would be cooking and not really praying. He said that I can get a hotel, so I got one for Friday, Saturday and check out on Sunday. I brought my bible and a case of water and anointing oil. I kept the TV off. I anointed myself and made petition of what I wanted prayers answered for. I wanted to fast and pray for our son, who had called and said he might be getting 60 years 20 years on three crimes. I didn't want that for our son and wanted to fast and pray. I really didn't know how to pray for our son. I knew that if I ask the Lord to set him free, he will go back to drinking and

taking drugs. So, I prayed Lord I don't want my son to be in jail for 60 years, and I don't even want him to spend a day there, but I know he'll go back to his ways. So, I told God do your will, but don't give him 60 years. I also prayed for my sisters to be set free from alcohol. My son ends up getting 5 years and 3 at the most for good time. One of my sisters was set free from alcohol in one month the other took her six months. Hallelujah! So I was driving home and had to drive through 4th Avenue in Anchorage. As I was driving the Lord said in an instant you see how full this is when people gather here for Fur Rondy and Iditarod? This is how it's going to be when people will come to know me as Lord and Savior. The street will be packed people coming to know our Lord and Savior. God is going to pour out his spirit on all flesh. Hallelujah! I believe God rewards you and shows you his plan when we fast and pray. When we hunger and thirst after righteousness. Later, after going to jail one more time our son finally gave his heart to the Lord. When he called and said he was going to jail I didn't cry or get mad, I was praising God and knew he was going to do something that he would change my son. Sure, enough my son accepted the Lord. The rest is my son's testimony. I don't want to say more he can tell his side. All those years while he was on drugs, I prayed for our son Lord watch over him send angels to protect him, protect his heart, lungs, kidneys. When I was fasting and praying the first day, I didn't really feel the presence of the Lord. I was making petitions. The second day oh man I was in battle I felt the presence of God and I was doing warfare. Breaking chains and moving in the spirit. Hallelujah! Thank you, Jesus! Today my son is traveling and sharing his testimonies. He has some powerful testimonies too. Before all this happened, when my son got out of prison a scary feeling had tried to creep on me. I prayed and asked the Lord to protect us. He said I don't need to be afraid of my son. I just need to accept him as he is and love him. I thought no one else will take care of him the way we can. He won't have a job and so no place to stay. So, we took him and let him stay with us. When he got out of prison he was on hard drugs like meth. All that time he was with us I prayed for him and took care of him. I didn't kick him out. Some days we end up in hotels to run away from him. If we let him move out, he'll be in the streets, and I was thinking no kid of mine will live in the streets. It was a very bumpy road of his recovery, but God took care of us and our son. I believe because of us being faithful to God and loving our son he didn't do any harm to us, without pointing fingers at him for what he was doing to us he got delivered and saved. All the glory goes to our loving Father who taught me how to love. He taught me to look at people that are miserable and who are mad at me for no reason to have compassion on them, because they are hurting inside and have no way to let the hurt out but to hurt others.

Psalm 37:4 Delight thyself also in the Lord; and he shall give thee the desires of thine heart.

Matthew 6:8 Be not ye therefore like unto them: for your Father knoweth what things ye have need of, before ye ask him.

Before we move to Anchorage, we were living in Delta Junction. I knew it was time to move and I prayed Lord if you are moving us to Point Hope provide tickets for us. If you are moving us to Anchorage to be with my parents provide a place to stay. So, I prayed God I know rent is high, and I don't want to pay a big rent. It says to be specific in your prayers. I want a 3–4-bedroom house and I want to pay 750 a month or even free I will not limit you. I left it at that. I went to my email a week later. I opened it and got an email from my cousin. She said she's looking for someone to watch their house just pay utilities. I said I'm looking I'll ask my husband. He was working in Point Lay at that time or in Prudhoe. I call and ask him he said go ahead. So, we packed and move. I now know what the word means don't ever say never. I used to say if we ever move to Anchorage, I'll never ever live in Mountain View area. So, for 8 years or so we lived rent free in a 4-bedroom house. God is good and answers prayers. What he did for me he can do for you amen! Don't limit him, don't say never ever haha. The place we lived in I prayed for angels to watch over us and ask God to put a hedge of protection over us. Lot of things happened in that area all around us, people tell us their property were stolen. We had a shed out there with expensive stuff and we never locked the door, but nothing was ever taken. Hallelujah! God is so good!

One time this is the year my husband didn't work almost a whole year while living in Delta. He learned to make baleen baskets in Anchorage. So, when he didn't work, he made baskets. We went to Fairbanks to sell his basket and during the winter it's very hard to sell, because it's not tourist season. We went to sell, we had a granddaughter, and her parents were in Fairbanks going to college. She needed diapers and we didn't want to bother the parents. So, we drove to Fairbanks from Delta. We went to practically all the little gift stores and everyone was like no we are not buying. We were getting desperate. The last place we were going to check I said you go in yourself I'll wait in the car. I prayed and I started worshipping a song came to my mind I started singing Pass Me Not Oh, Oh Gentle Savior. I was singing the chorus Savior, Savior hear my humble cry while on others thou art calling do not pass me by. That chorus had a different meaning to me that day. Savior, Savior hear my humble cry while on others thou blessing do not pass me by. I was singing with my whole hear and crying out to the Lord. Ira came out smiling he was coming towards the car, and I knew he sold it. He went into the car. Gave me the check and we were so thankful. He kept saying good thing I thought of this place. I knew it was the Lord that prompt him to go to that gift shop. I thanked the Lord so much for his blessing. We were able to get the diapers for

our granddaughter that day plus more. I think we left our granddaughter with her aunts at Delta I can't really remember, but I remember we needed diapers. Hallelujah God my provider. Jehovah Jireh!

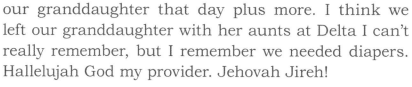

1 Peter 1:18 Forasmuch as ye know that ye were not redeemed with corruptible things, as silver and gold, from your vain conversations received by traditions from your fathers; 19 But with the precious blood of Christ, as of a lamb without blemish and without spot:

One year my sister and brother in-law caught a whale, was in the early 2000's. We had gone there to whale hunt with them. Ira went on the ice and that night it was getting a little windy and the captain wanted to go home. My husband said no we will be ok just stay a little while more. Good thing my husband wanted to stay they caught a whale. We were so blessed. They were cutting it and when we were at the head part a lot of the crews that were helping left. It was getting late at night and the crew decided we will go home and rest but leave two here to watch for the night. So, we were driving home, and I remembered my bag it had little stuff in there not much. When I remembered it, I said I plead the blood of Jesus over it. I just said Lord I forgot my bag and I plead the blood over it amen. We went home to rest and got home. We had left two guys there to watch the tent. We went back down to the camp, and a guy met us, and said we don't know what happened we can't explain it, Martha. I asked what happened? He said go look. Oh man my heart sank the tent burned down. Everything burned down one of the guys had left for town. We had a homemade wood stove. He put in a lot of wood and left the other sleeping. We think that a spark went on the tent and started the fire. It had all burned even the plywood flooring burn. The wooden grub box, what my dad made burned too. Good thing the guy sleeping was ok. We saw my bag it was in a carboard box and only the handle burned a little. The carboard box it was in didn't burn hallelujah! The one carboard box next to it full of other stuff burned. I remember the box next to it because I took a picture of a lady helping us cook in the tent and behind her was the two carboard boxes. Hallelujah to the Lamb of God! For his blood is so powerful. The guy that said we don't know how it happened meant everything burned but not my bag. Also, the contents in the box that it was in didn't burn. The cardboard box that was next to it burned. Jesus' blood is so powerful that nothing can come and harm or do anything when it has the blood covered. It was so amazing, I really should of plead the blood over the tent, but God wanted to show me how powerful his

Son Jesus' blood is. Hallelujah we are covered by the blood of the Lamb. Thank you, Jesus.

Exodus 15:26 And said, If thou wilt diligently hearken to the voice of the LORD, thy God, and wilt do that which is right in his sight, and wilt give ear to his commandments, and keep all his statutes, I will put none of these diseases upon thee, which I have brought upon the Egyptians: for I am the LORD that healeth thee.

Isaiah 53:5 But he was wounded for our transgressions, he was bruised for our iniquities: the chastisement of our peace *was upon him; and with his stripes we are healed.*

One year we were whaling, and the weather was getting bad. We had to rush and pack and go home. The crew packed and my sister and I packed the dishes and stuff inside the tent. The guys had snowmachines and my sister and I drove a four-wheeler. We were going and we hit a little ice that was higher like a step up. We stopped so suddenly and hard as I was driving, my sister was sitting behind me she went forward fast and hard and made my wrist bend so fast and hard under the handle. I hurt so bad, and I knew something was wrong. I kind of think it was broken. When I felt better, we kept going. I never got it checked. I was thinking it will heal. One day I was carrying a grocery bag full of stuff with the hand of the same side wrist that I injured and just like that it fell out of my hand. Sometime later, a crew from the church Oregon went to Point Hope Episcopal church to minister. I went there a whole bunch of us from the church went there. This guy asked whoever want to get prayed for come up and get prayed for I went up and they prayed for me, and I fell and while I was laying there my hand with injured wrist felt like I had to lift it up as I laid there on the floor. I surrendered and raised my hand. Then I started feeling heat around my wrist going so fast. The heat was going in circles around my wrist. I just laid there and let it happen. Oh, I was in so much awe. When it ended a guy came to me and asked me what was happening to me as I laid there. I told him

I had injured my wrist not too long ago and told him how it happened. I told him about the fire like that was going in circles around my wrist. We just praised God and thanked him. After that evening my wrist never hurt any more. My right wrist was healed hallelujah.I don't know how many years later I had a cyst on my hand, I can't remember if it was on my thumb joint or my pinky side, but it was on the same side of my injured wrist. This time I went to clinic, and they sent me to Kotzebue for x-ray. It happened for a purpose, so I got an x-ray on it. When I got done the doctor asked me if I ever broke my wrist, I told him I don't know but, I injured it before and told him about it. He said it has a scar and looks like I had broken it before. Hallelujah to the Lamb of God! My God my healer. You are worthy to be praised.

All these years God showed me so many things to glorify him and so many things that he did for me for his glory. When you believe him and please him he can show you great and mighty things. Never limit him. Yes we never limit our God he is the miracle worker.

Isaiah 30:21 and thine ears shall hear a word behind thee saying, This is the way, walk ye in it, when ye turn to the right hand, and when ye turn to the left.

John 10:27 My sheep hear my voice, and I know them, and they follow me:

He can tell you to do things and sometimes you think it's not that important. One day the church where I went to said we need to walk around the town and pray for the people. So, we walked around the whole town and when we got close to this house of an elderly named Sophie I said let's go in and go pray for her. She was so thankful she said she was so lonely and had been praying for someone to come and pray with her. We were so blessed when we found out she been praying for someone to come and see her. Hallelujah God is so loving!

Isaiah 41:10 Fear thou not; for I am with thee: be not dismayed; for I am thy God: I will strengthen thee; yea, I will help thee; yea I will uphold thee with the right hand of my righteousness.

Jeremiah 29:11 For I know the thoughts that I think toward you, saith the LORD thoughts of peace, and not of evil, to give you an expected end.

1 Peter 5:7 Casting all your care upon him; for he careth for you.

This is what I wrote on Facebook- 10/24/22 We had quite the experience last night. We left Whitehorse in the morning and got close to Watson Lake. All the way we were hoping we wouldn't run out of gas. No gas stations for miles. We found one and gassed up. So, we decided to eat at Watson Lake. We were leaving and same thing we saw on the way a sign that said check your gas. Oh, oh same thing as we were leaving Whitehorse, maybe no gas for miles. Anyways we took off. Siri took us the long dangerous route. We end up running out of gas in the middle of the boonies. I had been praying Lord stretch our gas, send your angels to us. We watched the gas stretch long ways, then suddenly it was using a lot of gas and I told Ira don't let it run out stop when we have at least enough for one mile. Long before that when the gas gauge was showing 130 miles before out, when we were turning from Robert Campbell Road to South Canol. I saw a big sign but couldn't read what it said. Ira just kept going and I said maybe we should go back and read what it says. We must has wasted like 12 miles worth of gas, by turning around to read the sign. So, we kept going and the road was getting narrow, rocky, steep and had some areas like blocked with trees, some areas with water puddles. We had to keep going or run out of gas if we even turn back. No traffic only one truck and a little car passed by us earlier, I think it was before turning from Robert Campbell to South Canol they passed us. As we were going, I was praying Lord stretch our gas and while we were going on the road, I would feel like something pushing us from the back of the truck and I was imaging angels pushing us. God stretched our gas to where he wanted us to go and he made it run out of gas fast where he wanted us to stop. Hallelujah! So, we end up running out of gas about 60 miles before the turning to the highway. I opened the window of the truck and hollered as loud as I can help!!! I can hear my echo go so far. It seems so hollow, and I can hear a river flowing. I was thinking we got drinking water nearby if we needed it. We finished our two bottles of water. I had packed some little snacks like pilot bread crackers and candy. When we were in Watson Lake restaurant before we left, I bought two bottles of water, Ira had some soda. We end sleeping a little in the truck. Praying and staying warm. Finally got brighter, about 8am. I heard like a four-wheeler or something like that. I got excited and pointed to the hazard light button. Hey, hey look! In the dark he found the button and went out to stop them.

It was two men a father and his son, they were riding on a side by side. We told them we ran out of gas and talked awhile. Then the father said he's got two jerry jugs of gas he said he can give us. I said we can buy the gas from him. So, they went to get the gas and the son gassed us up. We were so happy we were praising God. So happy of all places someone was there. Remember when we turned back to see the sign and when the gas gauge went so fast? It was all the Lord we ran out of gas not even a mile away from them. If we ran out of gas further up, we probably wouldn't see them in their RV because they were parked off the road on the left side. We'd pass by them and when they go hunting with side by side, we wouldn't see them. We didn't know it, but God had it all under control. Hallelujah! When we turned back to look at the sign, I wasn't too sure if we should turn back, because we would waste that precious gas. Hallelujah our footsteps are ordered by the Lord. We didn't have no connection on the phone. When I reported emergency, I should have pressed the report accident and not the hazard something. I accidently clicked out of my maps. I tried doing the SOS emergency button, but nothing happened it couldn't go out. Praise God there was these two-hunting moose. The guy said, they were late hunters, everyone is done hunting and shouldn't be there. He just had to try since they didn't get any moose. I prayed they got blessed with a moose. God is still on the throne and Jesus is sitting on the right hand of God interceding for us. We are seated in heavenly places with him. Hallelujah and amen! I praise him and I am still thankful till today. I was in a place in my mind, so this is how it is when people leave this world. I prayed even let people be praying for us. Our time is not yet, and the Lord is still going to use us for his glory. He showed us his glory and power that night and day. I cried and thanked the Lord. During that time on the road Ira was agreeing with me when I was praying. He was praying out loud. Hallelujah! Thank you, Jesus my Savior!

Jeremiah 17:14 Heal me, O LORD, and I shall be healed; save me, save me and I shall be saved: for thy art my praise.

September 2021, we end up with covid. Ira ends up in the hospital. When the ambulance came to pick him up and take him, they were taking him out the door the Lord said he is coming back home. I kept that promise in my heart. I end up being sick with fever, no appetite, no strength and later found out I had no taste. I had coughed up so much phlegm I made a little trash can full of Kleenex looked like a bouquet. It really looked like a bouquet, and it had a green store bag that made it even looked more real. I didn't really eat much few days and I told myself I need to even eat a little. I didn't know I lost my smell and taste. I realized it when my son was making pancakes and usually the fumes from the pancakes on the stove gives me allergy. I was telling myself I need to get good so I can fast and pray for my husband. I finally had strength and was being back to normal took me like

3 days or so. I told my son I'm not eating I'm going to fast and pray for your dad. I fasted that morning and prayed. I shut our bedroom door, got my bible ready, got my oil and anointed myself. I started praying scriptures over Ira and I was speaking life over him. I felt I was pushing the spirit of death away from him. Every time I prayed, I felt I was pushing inch by inch the spirit of death. Thank you, Jesus! I don't know how many days later a guy from the hospital called me and asked me how I was doing. He asked me questions and I asked him questions of how long I should quarantine and all that. Every time I hear of Ira not doing good, I would pray for him. I was in a battle spiritually. They kept in touch with me on Ira. I was able to speak to him. Every time I asked how he was he would say I'm doing good. We missed each other's so much, because we never been away from one another for so long. Before we hang up, we would say I love you and it wasn't from the mouth it came from the heart. Those words absence makes the heart grow fonder are very true. I was told I couldn't go see him, because they weren't letting any visitors to the hospital and only time anyone can come to visit is to say your goodbyes. I heard from someone when your taken with ambulance that's the time they put them on breathing machines or something like that. I got a call and was told I can go see him, they said that he was getting worst. I wouldn't accept it and I called our daughters. I told them I don't believe what they are saying. My daughters all said I don't believe it either. We all prayed three of our daughters were in Anchorage, one in Wasilla, one in Kenai and one in Point Hope. Five of them said they were going to drive to Fairbanks and I said I would drive from Delta Junction.

I got to Fairbanks and I called and told them I was here to see my husband. This lady sounded confused and said what are you talking about. He can't have any visitors only time is when he is not doing good, and he looks fine. I told her I drove from Delta Junction and you guys said I can go visit him. She finally said since you came all the way from Delta we will let you come and see him. I asked how about our daughters they are on the way from Anchorage and Kenai they said they can come and see him two at a time. So, we got to see him. I prayed for my husband. He told me that he quit getting up to walk, because every time he got up his breathing would get short, and they would double his breathing stuff. They would put a nasal canula and a mouthpiece with full force. That's how he got better he quit getting up to walk. The nurses said he wasn't eating, and I asked if I should make him our native food, I made him something simple and he didn't eat that. I got him fast food and still he wasn't eating, So, I was thinking when I was sick and when I don't have appetite what did I want to eat. When I was sick and had no appetite all I wanted was junk food. So, my granddaughter and I got him some food he like to eat. We got him pepsi, wheat thins crackers, raisins, pilot bread crackers, canned apricot, and a lot more I forgot. He started eating wheat thins and started drinking pepsi. After that he got his appetite, he started to finish his food the hospital was feeding him. The Lord gets all the glory he will give you wisdom. Later, they told me he can get out but, needed to stay near a hospital. So, they asked me to look for a place. I started to look and most of the places wanted a year lease, and I didn't want to stay in Fairbanks. We wanted to move closer to

our children in Anchorage. I looked and looked couldn't find anything. I got a call from the nurses saying he is getting out in a day or two. I didn't find a place to stay and needed to find a place I asked my husband if he can stay in the hospital till Monday, but he wanted to go out so bad. So that night I prayed and by faith I applied for Airbnb for a whole month. The next morning it was a Saturday and still hadn't heard from the Airbnb, by faith I drove to Fairbanks. I was praying on the way to Fairbanks and I felt the Lord saying pray now in tongues. I prayed in tongues and faith arose and I knew something good happened in the spirit. Hallelujah to the Lamb of God! I by faith went to a grocery store in North Pole. I was thinking I needed to buy food, because no one will go to the store for me. I needed to shop before Ira gets to the place. They said they would bring him to wherever they needed to with ambulance. I parked in the parking place looked at my Airbnb and I got a message, and the lady answered and said they approved my place to stay. I started crying and praising God. I was walking into Safeway with tears in my eyes and I didn't care if anyone saw me. If they asked me, I would tell them happy tears to my heavenly Father. My Father God, my Abba Father, my provider had heard and provided and paved the way. Hallelujah oh the joy was so much and the thankfulness. I could have cried a ton of tears, but I had to go buy food and little things for our place to stay in North Pole. I was almost running and shopping smiling from ear to ear. So, I bought the food and went to the place. I don't know how long it was that I was in the place, and they called and said they were on the way. I decided to order food on DoorDash. I ordered food and waited it said it was delivered, but I didn't get anything. So I looked up the address I put in. I had put in the wrong address I went to look for the address and didn't find it. So, I was thinking I better head back. When I got back the ambulance was waiting, they brought Ira. They were so happy to see me I told the ambulance crew that I was ordered on DoorDash and didn't get it that I put in the wrong address. They chuckled and I did too. They were just happy I got there. They brought Ira in and got him all settled with the oxygen and all. We stayed there a few days then the hospital people were talking about getting a place in Fairbanks. I told them we wanted to move to Anchorage where our daughters were and wanted to stay closer to family. They agreed and started working on the move. I told them I can't take him on a long drive with the oxygen and it was a long drive for him. They agreed it was a long drive with oxygen, so they worked on it and brought him to Anchorage with LifeMed they set up everything. They picked him up with ambulance took him to airport to the LifeMed plane. Then picked him up from the airport in Anchorage with ambulance. They got it all set up where we stayed in a place provided by ASNA. They made sure someone was there at the place to meet him. One of our daughters met them at the place. The hospice had it all set for him to have oxygen at the place. Our daughter bought everything that we needed coffee and food, had it already for us. We had asked one of our daughters to come to Fairbanks so she can drive me to Delta Junction and pick up our clothes and stuff that we will need in Anchorage. We road from Fairbanks to Delta Junction spent the night and then drove to Anchorage. God is so good he made sure

everything that needed to be done was done. Ira was told that he would be on oxygen all the rest of his life and was on hospice. They gave him amount of time to live on earth, but God had other plans. Hallelujah! I took care of him from November to May. I had to make coffee for him, feed him when the nurse quit coming to give him bathes, I gave him bathes. I had to change the oxygen from high to low every time he gets up, I turn it up and every time he settles downs when his oxygen goes up on its own I turn the oxygen down. One day I was thinking if I got sick who would care for him. No one can care for him like I do. I know what he needs and what need to be done. No one can read his mind like in what he wants and stuff like that. Being together so many years I can tell it in his eyes. All that time I didn't get sick. Hallelujah God made sure. There were days I laid hands on him while he was sleeping asking God to heal him. One time he wasn't breathing too good while he was sleeping. I was praying for his niece and him. That time so many people needed to be prayed for. I asked God even I know that God felt what we were going through. I asked God do you feel what I'm feeling, do you feel the hurt too? I really wanted to hear from God. He gave me Proverbs 3: 5 and 6 Trust in the Lord with all thine heart; and lean not unto thine own understanding. 6 In all thy ways acknowledge him, and he shall direct thy path. I got so blessed and said OK Lord, I trust you. We will go through this just for a moment. Something good is going to happen. I believe it's not always going to be like this. I felt it in my spirit that Ira will be ok. Also, for our niece she will be ok. When God speaks it always gets done. We end up staying in hospice from November till May. I was able to go out and do a little, he was able to drive. He felt so set free when he was able to drive. It wasn't long after in June we went home he walked through those doors not completely out of the oxygen but slowly getting out of it. Remember when the Lord told me that he will come home again that he will be back? I held on to the promise the Lord gave me. Satan tried to lie to us, and we never believed. We believed that my husband would live and make it through this covid. We didn't receive anything the doctor told us. When the doctor said he will always have to use oxygen I said to that doctor that oxygen has to go in the name of Jesus! Hallelujah to the Lamb of God! Today Ira doesn't need the oxygen. There was a time before he got covid a year and a half before that he got sick almost didn't make it. He was on oxygen because his lungs got damaged from years of smoking, they couldn't really tell what triggered it. He ended up using the oxygen and the nurse said this is your baby now, meaning the oxygen. I said nope that baby must leave in the name of Jesus! He got out of the oxygen. Not too long after that. We never accepted what the doctors said to us. We know we have a God that says the last word.

John 8:32 And you shall know the truth, and the truth shall make you free.

You know the truth will set you free. I had always had migraine headaches for years. One day I went to get seen for it and the doctor told me I had fibromyalgia. I

went home and looked up the definition of fibromyalgia. I was reading it, and it says can be from past trauma. I had a lot of things happened to me when I was young to my adult life that were so traumatizing. I was like I don't have to live this life like in pain. It's not me and I won't let it define me. I claimed that God had healed me. That the truth has set me free. After that no more headaches. When I heard what the doctor told me I didn't accept it. That's not the truth about me it's a lie straight from the pits of hell. Hallelujah, he set me free. I don't have any more migraines. Hallelujah! The bible is the truth it never lies. It gives life, it heals, its everything in life that you need. It is the breath that you breathe. That is the Word of God. He is the Word, the truth and the life. Hallelujah.

Writing this book took me a long time to finish this. I had started somewhere around 2003 or something like that I can't remember. I had quit writing when I couldn't do it anymore. I was going to write more of all the years I was traumatized growing up, but I couldn't do it every time I started writing I'd start crying. So, I quit writing and it always been on the back of my head I need to write the testimonies down and share. Till one day I was writing and sharing on Facebook, and someone said to me Martha you need to write a book of how to pray. She said you don't have to write everything that happened in your life. I never told her anything of that I had started writing. I knew it was the Lord using her to go forward on the book. I shared a lot of places when I had a chance, when church is happening, and the mike is open for testimony and singing. I would share whatever the Lord wants me to share on. I know

I shared out of your belly shall flow rivers of living water a lot of times where the Lord wanted me to share. One time I shared in a place they don't believe tongues should happen today. I didn't know that they were one to never allow it, but anyways I shared. The leader I was traveling with said to me Martha you're going to share tonight. We will call on you when it's your turn. I share when I first got fill. Hallelujah! There was a young guy up front that shed a tear when I shared. I found out about they didn't believe about speaking in tongues later the next few days after we left that village. The guy told me, and he was like Martha, you almost got us kicked out. He was joking and laughing. It was the Lord that put it in my heart to share this testimony. When the leader told me I needed to share I was like what am I going to share and this testimony of out of your belly shall flow rivers of living water keep coming to my mind. That's what the Lord wanted me to share, and I did it. Hallelujah! It's a good thing I didn't' know they don't speak in tongues I probably wouldn't share it if I knew. I know these testimonies that the Lord gave us are not our own, but they are testimonies to be shared. The Lord works in us in all different ways. Some may never experience what I did, and some have. God works in us for his glory! Hallelujah! I shared these testimonies in a lot of places. Whenever there is an opening for me to share. A lot of places that I go when it is an open mike to share, they give you a time limit. So, I don't get to share a lot, but if the Lord wants me to share I will. Hallelujah to the Lamb of God for always being there to show me his great and mighty works. He did it all so that he can get all the glory, honor and

praise. What he has done for me he can do it for all. I started writing this book many years ago. Might have been 2003 or earlier or later. I quit writing, but the Lord kept reminding me to get it done. He wants us to give him the glory in our lives. He has done so much in our lives. I still praise him today and thank him each day for everything because he is worthy of it all. All these testimonies are the truth, and it all happen for a purpose. We cannot limit God in what he can do. We need to trust his word. Believe he can do it, be hungry for his word and a new refreshing touch. He can work in you through you and around you. He is able, when I can't do it, he does it for me. I hope this book encourages you to live a life with the Lord, because with him there is healing, blessings, and many more things that he can show us.

Today if you never receive Jesus as your Lord and Savior now is the time. Jesus is coming soon. We can see it today times have changed. Thanks for reading my testimonies what the Lord gave me to share for his glory. In this book God gets all the glory. It's hard to end these stories of my testimonies. I don't know how to end it, because my testimonies are not ended. Hallelujah! Thank you Jesus!

Me and My Husband

Abe Leo Zoey papa and aaka

Baby Ebrulik winning
baby contest and his dad

Claudia, grandkids and papa

Crystal and sons Kobe Jaden
Brayden and Franklin Granddaughter
Ari Claudia s daughter

Daughter Annette

Daughter Claudia and family

Daughter Emma

Daughter Maxine and son in law Drew

Ebrulik who passed

Ebrulik our grandson but calls us mom
and dad. Named after our son who passed

Eldest daughter Helen and Leon

Eldest daughter Helen

Grand baby Martha

Granddaughter Angelica
with papa and aaka

Granddaughter Becky with papa and aaka

Granddaughter Charla with papa and aaka

Grandkids

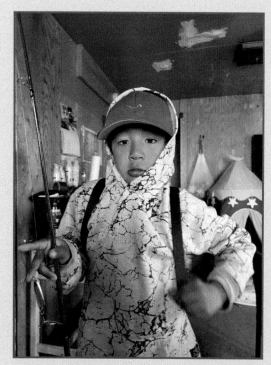

Grandson Seymour

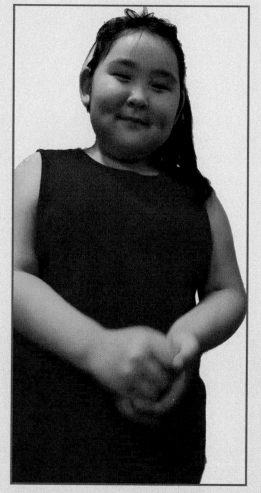

Great Granddaughter Renezmae

Great grandson

Hubby Ira and
grandson Milton

Ira Jr and part of his family

Hubby Ira on blanket toss

Me and daughters

Me on the blanket toss the year we caught a whale. Whaling feast 2015

Me praising God in musicale. Photo by Bill Hess

Me, Kendra, Abraham and papa

Mom and dad with our adult kids

our daughters Helen, Crystal holding
her son Brayton, Maxine and family

Our son Ebrulik

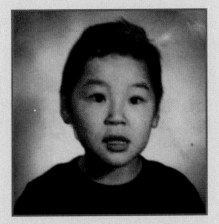

Our son Ebrulik this picture
was taken before he passed

Papa and granddaughters

Us and grandkids

Grand baby Lucy

Grand baby Martha

Daughter Maxine

Printed in the United States
by Baker & Taylor Publisher Services